We Serve, Too!

A Child's Deployment Book

Written and Illustrated by **Kathleen Edick** and **Paula J. Johnson**

Author
Dedications

Dedicated
with a salute to
Devon Victoria and Landon Bradley,
their soldier Dad and brave Mom
--one family of thousands
of proud
military tradition.

- Kathleen Edick-

With
Gratitude
to my heroes
--America's "littlest" Patriots,
who love through their loneliness,
serve through their separations,
and bravely share with us
their soldier dads
in defense of our country.
Be proud little brave ones.

-Paula Johnson

© 2007
We Serve Too!
www.weservetoo.us
Printed in Korea
All Rights Reserved
Formatting and Design by
REdesign Studios
www.ryanedesigns.com

In humble recognition
of the proud men and women
serving in the U.S. Military;
hailing from different states
and different cultures,
serving in different branches
and different capacities,
stationed and deployed
in different places around the world;
...yet one
in determined purpose
to
KEEP US FREE.

M y daddy joined the Army
        He's away from me and Mommy;
and I don't like it...

-NOT ONE BIT!

Sometimes
    I even pitch a fit;

And sometimes...

Daddy's unit was deployed
His work is far away;
    and though we are not overjoyed,
A soldier must obey.

The Army said we couldn't go
    and Dad said, "Stay right here,
And wait for me 'till I get back
    in just about a year."

Sometimes when Dad is far away he's in a danger zone,

And that is why he wants us here

-safe and sound at home.

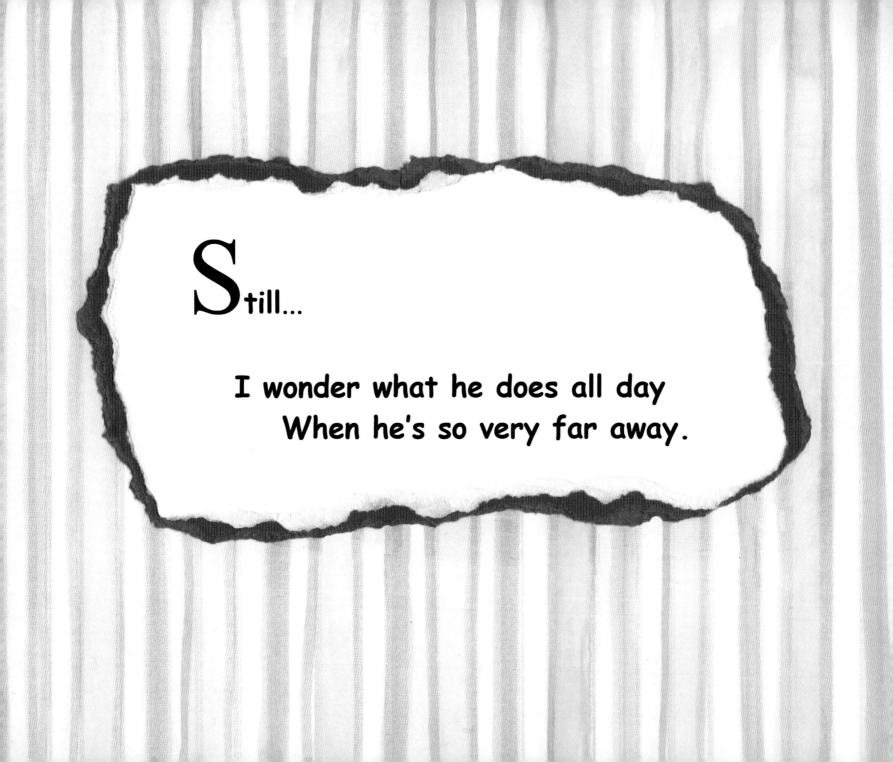

Still...

I wonder what he does all day
    When he's so very far away.

I think of him when I get up;

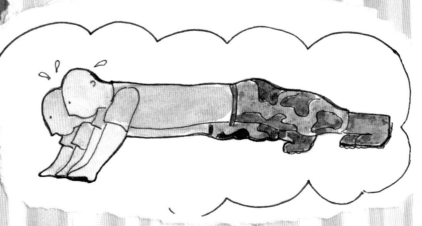

I think of him at play;

Digging holes...

On the fly!

Private Eye!

And now,
   when it is time to eat,
I wonder...
   does he get a treat?
Does he say,
   "May I?" and "Please?"

I rest my head each afternoon
    and wish that Dad would get home soon.
He said deployment would be rough...

But we'll be fine

-our family's TOUGH!

M ost other dads come home at night,
But mine's too far away.

He's fighting hard
in freedom's fight.

He loves our USA.

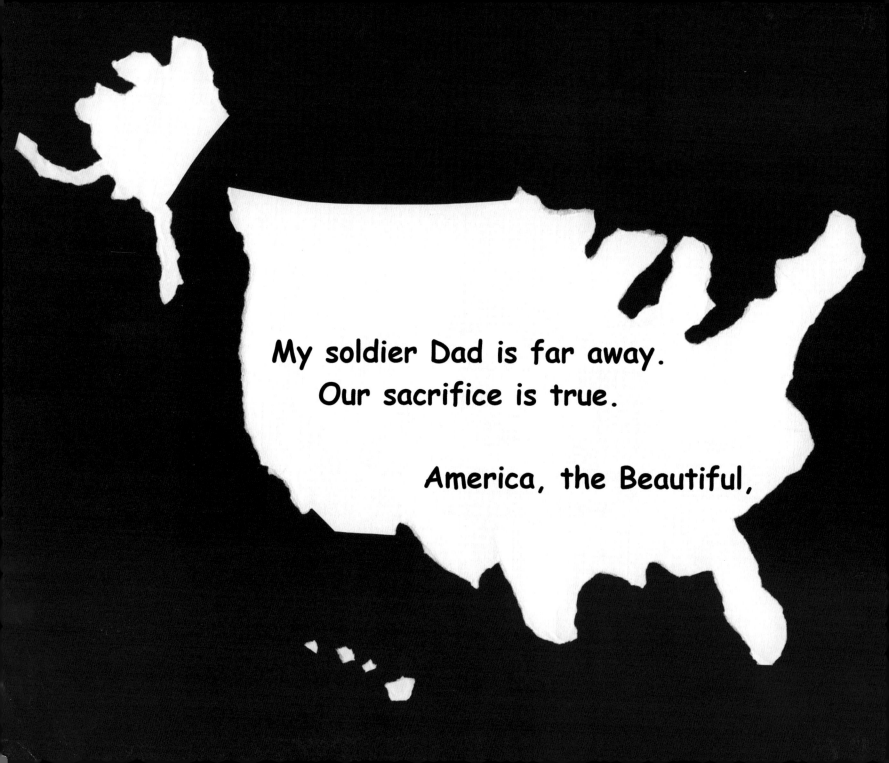

My soldier Dad is far away.
Our sacrifice is true.

America, the Beautiful,

It's nighttime now...

I feel so sad.
At bedtime I most miss my Dad.

I say my prayers before I sleep
  and ask that God will hold and keep
him safe from harm, and make him strong
  and give him faith to fight the wrong.

And Daddy says he does the same. He prays for us each night,

That we'll be safe and brave and strong and always do what's right.

My mama needs a hug tonight;
She'd like one from my dad.
    I'll give her one for both of us
So she won't be so sad.

And now I snuggle down to sleep.
    Oh, Mama, tuck me tight.
Snug me up like Daddy's hug

    We'll all sleep tight tonight.

...Goodnight...